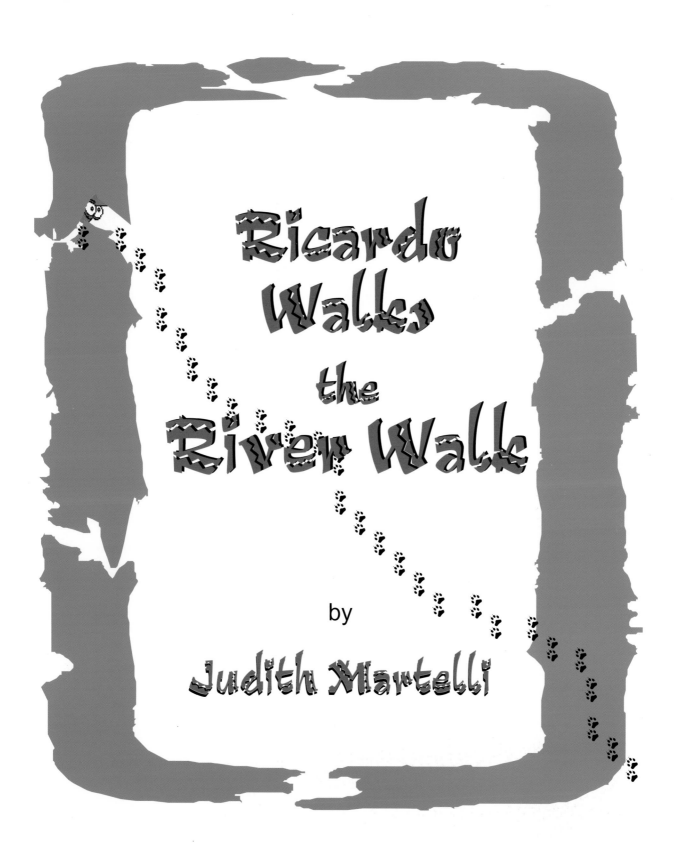

Ricardo Walks the River Walk

by

Judith Martelli

EAKIN PRESS ★ Austin, Texas

For my mother

FIRST EDITION

Copyright © 1998
By Judith Martelli

Published in the United States of America
By Eakin Press
A Division of Sunbelt Media, Inc.
P.O. Drawer 90159
Austin, TX 78709-0159
1-800-880-8642

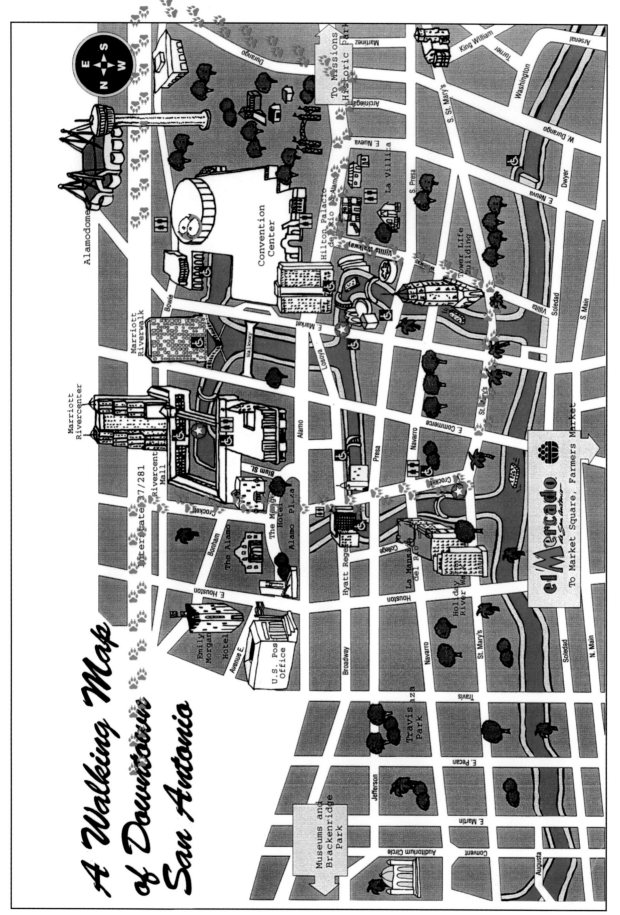

Map courtesy of *Paseo del Rio.*

Judith Martelli, a native San Antonian, presents her love for this beautiful city in her books and photographs. She shares the beauty and joy of San Antonio's famed River Walk with readers of all ages. You are invited to come join in the celebration and happy times that await all who come to this most special place. There is, indeed, an exciting adventure around every bend in the river's winding path.

As you read through the book,

see how many times you can find Ricardo hiding on each page.

Look for the answer in the back.

Ricardo felt lucky
to live in
San Antonio.
The city was a very
exciting place.
It had many
tall buildings.

Some were old and
some were new.

It had many
historical
and
interesting
places to visit.

Photo courtesy of San Antonio Zoo, Mark Mayfield, Finger Prints, Inc.

This city was different because of one thing . . . it had a secret nestled below. A special place to escape the noisy streets.

One entered this special place by walking down the many old steps that descended from the world above.

This place was like no other. There was a milky green river which was the center of everything. It quietly wound its way through the big city above. It flowed under the many old stone bridges that arched themselves over it.

There were
lush
tropical plants
along the
riverbank,
and ivy draped
the old stone
walls.

Old cypress
trees
stretched tall
to the city
above.

9

They shaded
the river
and winding
walkways
below.

People came
from near and
far to visit this
beautiful place.

10

Ricardo was one of the furry little inhabitants who call the river home. Ricardo loved his home. The mornings were peaceful and quiet.

The sun beamed its warm rays to this world below, reflecting on the river in sparkling brilliance.

11

Pigeons
roosted
under the
old stone
bridges.

Ricardo
loved the gen-
tle cooing
sounds they
made. Rising
from the
silence of
early morning
sunshine, the
birdsong was
soothing to
his little soul.
Shops,
restaurants,
and big hotels
lined the
river's path.

12

This was a special place they called the River Walk. Brightly colored barges provided river transportation. People floated down the river for many reasons. Early morning would bring the working barges. They chugged along the river pathways with their mysterious cargo.

Ricardo would sit on the riverbank and wonder with great curiosity what magical contents the big boxes and cartons contained. Some had long hoses with special water pumps aboard.

Ricardo hid and watched as men took the long hoses and watered the many plants that grew along the river's banks. During the day sight-seeing barges would pass by.

The barges had little benches aboard for riders to relax on while enjoying the sights and scenery along the river's path.

14

People would wave from the bridges above as the barges passed below. They would pass the bustling sidewalk activities.

People could be seen having lunch at little outdoor tables with color-ful umbrellas.

Well-fed pigeons strolled under-neath the tables feasting on little tidbits that would generously fall their way. Look at these brave birds! They are feasting on the table!

The barges would pass schools of fish trying to retrieve little bits of food from children at the river's edge. They passed the many novelty shops loaded with treasure. Big hotels lined the river's path, and their large open doors beckoned a warm and friendly hello.

The river even
flowed through
one hotel lobby!
It went in the
front door and
out the
back door.
It continued on
past walls of
water and lush
vegetation.

At the end of the winding pathway was a huge waterfall. It roared down from the city streets above. Ricardo knew a little secret! If you climbed the steps beside the waterfall, something very special awaited above.

18

It was the ALAMO... the historical shrine of Texas! It was a place of honor where brave men stood their ground and changed the course of history.

Evening brought both sight-seeing and dinner barges. Dinner barges would float by with little candles flickering in the night. Happy sounds of laughter filled the air.

Photo courtesy of San Antonio Convention & Visitors Bureau, Craig Stafford

The barges passed an outdoor river theater. Spanish dancers could be seen twirling to lively Mariachi music on the river's stage. On the other side of the river were grassy terraced steps.

Crowds of people gathered to sit on the steps and enjoy the music and dancing. The gay spirited music filled the air as it drifted down the River Walk. Ricardo loved the festive music. It enriched his world and made him feel like dancing. His spirit soared!

It was mid-January and a chill was in the air. As night fell, Ricardo noticed a strange steam rising from the river. It blanketed the entire River Walk. The little tables and chairs along the sidewalk were empty. Where were all the people? Ricardo shivered as he tucked himself in for the night.

It was dawn when he awoke. He rubbed his eyes and gathered courage to peek outside. There was no river traffic in sight! He went to the bank and peered slowly over the edge. His stomach fell to his feet. His beloved river was missing something very important...WATER! In its place was an empty, muddy river bottom.

Ricardo heard men in the distance talking. He hid behind a bush and listened as their voices came closer. The men were walking in the muddy river bottom wearing tall rubber boots.

21

They seemed to be searching for something. He watched as they brought up broken dishes, a camera, a pistol, trash of all kinds, jewelry, money...even a huge *relic*. Ricardo guessed it must be a dinosaur jawbone! Were they finding *trash* or *treasure*? Day after day the workers sifted through the muddy river bottom.

As evening fell, the townsfolk seemed to celebrate the mud! They held a Mud Pie Ball and a Mud Coronation. They even crowned a Mud King and Queen!

Ricardo was very sad. He had decided he would never see his beautiful river again. Late one afternoon as the sun was casting long shadows on the riverbank, Ricardo was napping on his tree branch. Suddenly, he was awakened by a noisy procession. He peered down to the sidewalk below. The *strangest* parade he had ever seen was passing beneath him.

People were dressed in silly costumes and *bathrobes*. Some were wearing shower caps and rubber pig noses! They paraded down the side-walk, tossing gaudy beads and coins to the gathering crowds. There were floats that *didn't* float.

There was a pig dressed in a crazy costume being pulled in a little wagon. It was the silliest parade Ricardo had ever seen. *Mud-jorettes* and *mud bands* marched ahead. They were followed by the King and Queen of Mud wearing bathrobes and large silly crowns. The King was passing out wooden coins and trinkets to the spectators.

Ricardo decided to leave the safety of his tree and join in the frivolity of this zany *celebration* of mud! Along the way were mud fishing contests and trays full of mud. You could put your hands in the mud and make your very own mud pies! One restaurant even offered a tray of *mud food!*

Suddenly, Ricardo knew why they were all celebrating.
He had been wrong! It wasn't the mud at all! It was the *return* of his beloved river! Where had it been?

Ricardo overheard someone say that the river had been drained to clean the river bottom. Now they were opening the flood gates and letting the water and fish return.

It had certainly been a week filled with surprises. Ricardo had to admit that he had loved every muddy minute of it. But he was so happy that the river had finally returned.

Many special events happened along the River Walk each year. There was Mardi Gras with colorful masks and costumes. On St. Patrick's Day there was the Dyeing O' the River Green. Floats would release environmentally friendly green dye into the river. But there was one event Ricardo favored above all...**FIESTA**! Fiesta time was an especially happy occasion. Crowds gathered to share happy times and great food.

The River Walk was filled with noisy excitement. Children smashed firecracker noise-makers beneath their shoes with a big **BANG**!

Cascarones, colorfully painted hollow egg shells filled with confetti, were a Ricardo specialty! He loved to smash them over unsuspecting heads! Mariachi groups performed on decorated floating stages, and their music filled the air.

Ricardo's little tummy would be very round at Fiesta time for he had quite a passion for Mexican food. He would always *overindulge* himself until he rolled! **CARAMBA!** What a *delicious* life!

Photo courtesy of Fiesta San Antonio Commission, Inc.

The highlight of Fiesta was a river parade! Barges were decorated with brightly colored paper flowers and decorations. Men, women, and children were dressed in beautiful jeweled costumes.

At the beginning of the parade, King Antonio made his grand entrance on his royal barge. He was the King of Fiesta! He would wave to the crowds as his royal court followed him down the river.

Ricardo always viewed the parade from his special tree branch. It was spectacular! Ricardo felt secure that his life along the river would always be grand.

27

But *alas*...Ricardo was awakened one morning by strange noises. Workmen were setting up ladders along the River Walk. They were attaching long pieces of wire everywhere. Some of the men were setting little bags along the walkways and placing a mysterious object into each one.

Perhaps a fuse of some kind, thought Ricardo. One of the workmen said they would be *lighting* them soon! This scared little Ricardo.

A big machine was placed on the walkway. It had a handle and was hooked up to all the wires the men were attaching everywhere. He heard one of the workmen say that when the handle was lowered, it would **ALL GO OFF**!!! How dreadful!

One evening crowds of people started gathering. Ricardo had never seen so many people. Then the Mayor arrived. A strange hush of anticipation filled the air. Ricardo overheard someone say that **IT WOULD ALL GO OFF AT 7 O'CLOCK**!!!
He felt faint as he awaited the terrible fate. Why would people come to see something so beautiful be so *cruelly* destroyed?

Suddenly, Ricardo became aware that they had all begun counting:
10-9-8 Ricardo covered his little ears and closed his eyes tight.
7-6 He could not watch another minute of it!
5-4 What would happen when they ran out of numbers?
3-2 It was too horrible to imagine...those awful wires and fuses!

The dreaded moment had now arrived!

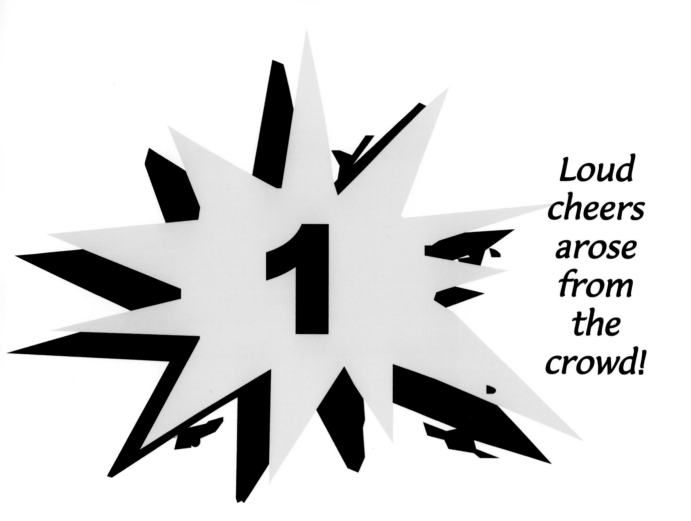

1

Loud cheers arose from the crowd!

Photo courtesy of San Antonio Convention & Visitors Bureau, Al Rendon

Ricardo did not hear an explosion. What was happening? He slowly opened his eyes. He could not believe what he saw! It was as if his beloved River Walk had been transformed into a fantasy beyond belief!

Every tree and bridge twinkled with little colored lights, creating a magical reflection in his beautiful river.
It was a fairyland of light...
a heavenly vision! He burst into little back flips of joy. This was more beautiful than he could endure!

Photo courtesy of San Antonio Convention & Visitors Bureau, Richard Reynolds

Photo courtesy of San Antonio Light Collection, UT Institute of Texan Cultures

One by one the little bags were lit along the walkway. The hidden secret inside each bag was a small candle set in sand. They were called *luminarias*.
Their flickering flames cast long, soft shadows of light over the river and walkway.

Decorated floats carrying carolers drifted by. The night air was filled with beautiful holiday music. This had to be the most beautiful night in the world, thought Ricardo.

30

This was the *holy season*, and his River Walk had been adorned with beautiful lights to celebrate this most blessed time of the year. It was the most precious gift anyone had ever given him. After all, life should be a joyful celebration.

Each passing day awakens to an exciting new adventure. It beckons to all: **COME!** Enjoy the beauty *unfolding* with each new passing day. Take a walk along the River Walk.

• • • • • • • • • • • • • •

Although Ricardo remains a mystery to all, his story is very special. What makes it so special is that it is about a very real River Walk in San Antonio, Texas. All of the special events that take place in Ricardo's little story really do happen there. He invites you to step from the pages of this story into the real excitement and beauty of the San Antonio River Walk. Happy times await you, and Ricardo will be looking for you!

Paseo Del Rio Events Calendar

January: Annual Mud Festival. The celebration features the Mud Pie Ball, Mud Coronation and Mud Parade. Great Country River Festival.

February: Mardi Gras. A festival of sidewalk parades and the Mardi Gras mini-parade of colorful floats cruise around the River Bend.

March: Dyeing O' the River Green Parade. Floats release over thirty pounds of environmentally friendly green dye into the river. The event transforms the 2.5-mile river into a miniature Emerald Isle.

April: Fiesta Mariachi Festival. Mariachi groups perform on decorated floating stages along the River Walk for Fiesta.

May: Kick-off to Summer...Memorial Day Weekend. Texas artisans present one-of-a-kind gifts along the River Walk. Canoe teams compete in timed heats in the Canoe Challenge through the central River Bend area of the River Walk.

September: Pachanga del Rio. Participants enjoy sampling culinary offerings of thirty participating restaurants.

Texas Country Festival. Live performances featuring country-western music presented at the Rivercenter Lagoon as well as on two floating stages.

October: Halloween Festival. "Downtown Haunts" street dance. A Halloween celebration featuring live music, food, drinks and a special dance performance. Enter the mysterious haunts of the River Walk as you witness the creepiest river parade ever..."Coffins on Parade"!

November and December: River Walk Parade and Lighting Ceremony. The switch is pulled, turning on over 80,000 colored lights illuminating the River Walk until New Year's. Decorated floats wind through the river in a nighttime river parade. Lighting at 7:00 P.M.

Holiday Boat Caroling. Holiday caroling fills the air as more than 185 groups cruise the River Walk area on decorated floats.

Fiesta de las Luminarias. The River Walk is ablaze with candlelight as more than 2,500 *luminaria* bags line the walkways to symbolically mark the "lighting of the way."

Rivercenter Christmas Pageant. Riverboats portraying the Christmas story float into the Rivercenter Lagoon. The classic nativity scene unfolds.

River Walk Art Fair. Artisans from Texas and the Southwest feature one-of-a-kind gifts.

Las Posadas. Candle-lit procession led by children costumed as members of the Holy Family search for an inn.

Ricardo appears 29 times.